My Picture
Art Class

Nellie Shepherd

A Dorling Kindersley Book

LONDON, NEW YORK, MUNICH, MELBOURNE, AND DELHI

Editor Penny Smith
Designer Jane Horne
Managing Art Editor Diane Thistlethwaite
Production Rochelle Talary
Photography Stephen Hepworth

For James Pendrich (My Wonderful Friend!)

ACKNOWLEDGEMENTS
With thanks to: Jean Gollner, Anne Lumb, Wendy Morrison,
James Pendrich, Melena and Megan Smart (MMKS Logistics), Joan Fallows,
David Hansel (Memery Crystal), and the children from Cressbrook Mill,
Abbeydale School, and Broomhall Nursery School and Early Years Centre.
Special thanks to the artists: Peggy Atherton,
Emma Guest, and Emma Hardy.

First published in Great Britain in 2003
by Dorling Kindersley Limited
80 Strand, London WC2R ORL
A Penguin Company
2 4 6 8 10 9 7 5 3 1

A CIP catalogue record for this book
is available from the British Library

ISBN: 1-4053-0083-3

Colour reproduction by GRB Editrice, Italy
Printed and bound in Italy by L.E.G.O.

See
Dorling Kindersley's
complete catalogue at
www.dk.com

Where to find things

My Picture Art Class

In this book we're creating brilliant pictures. And after each picture there's a 3-D project to make.

"Using bits and bobs creates really good bits and bobs," Anna, age five, once told me. This is the message of **My Picture Art Class**. Improvise, search around the house, and see what "bits" you can use to create your pictures – and your fabulous 3-D projects, including a Funky Fish hat and a Racy Rocket! Prepare yourself for sticky fingers and go for it!

Nellie Shepherd

Read Nellie's tips on page 46 and be inspired!

4

Basic Kit

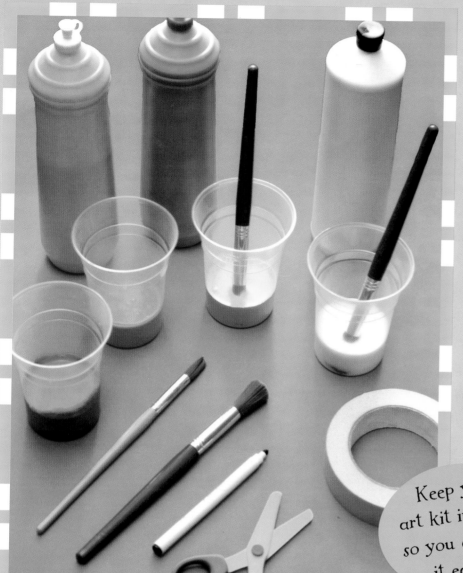

As well as the equipment pictured with each project, you will need the following basic kit:

card	stapler
paper	pots (for paint
paints	and glue)
felt-tip pens	paintbrushes
pencils	rollers
PVA glue	tissue paper
tape (masking	cotton wool
tape is best)	wool
scissors	beads

Keep your art kit in a box so you can find it easily!

Helping hand

All the projects in this book are designed for young children to make, but they should only be attempted under adult supervision. Extra care should be taken when using sharp equipment, such as scissors, staplers, and pipe cleaners, and with small objects that may cause choking. Only use PVA or other non-toxic, water-soluble glue.

Sea World

tissue paper

shiny button

6

Here's a lovely sparkly picture
Of the world under the sea.
With plants and little fishes,
It's a magical place to be.

You can use...

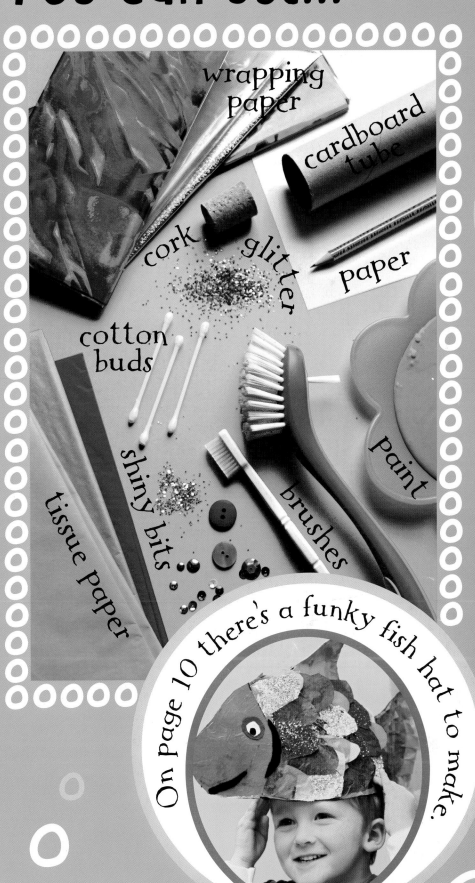

wrapping paper

cardboard tube

cork

glitter

paper

cotton buds

shiny bits

tissue paper

brushes

paint

On Page 10 there's a funky fish hat to make.

paint

How to make it!

draw

The first thing to do is to draw fish shapes, starfish, shells, or other designs on paper. Now cut them out.

decorate

Decorate your designs with wrapping paper, paint, glitter, and shiny bits so they look lovely!

Who's for chips?

paint

Use brushes or rollers to paint a sea background. Add water to the paint for a washy, watery look. Dab on paint with a cork or cotton buds for extra texture.

blob away!

To put bubbles in the sea, dip a cardboard tube in paint and blob away! Twist tissue paper to make seaweed, paint on swirls, and stick on more shiny bits. Add your fish and other designs.

Kid's talk
"The sea goes on forever."
Helena, age 4

Funky Fish

Isn't this a funky hat –
A fish up on your head!
You can wear it all day long,
But take it off for bed!

tissue paper

glitter

Wear me
on your
head!

Kitchen foil

You can use...

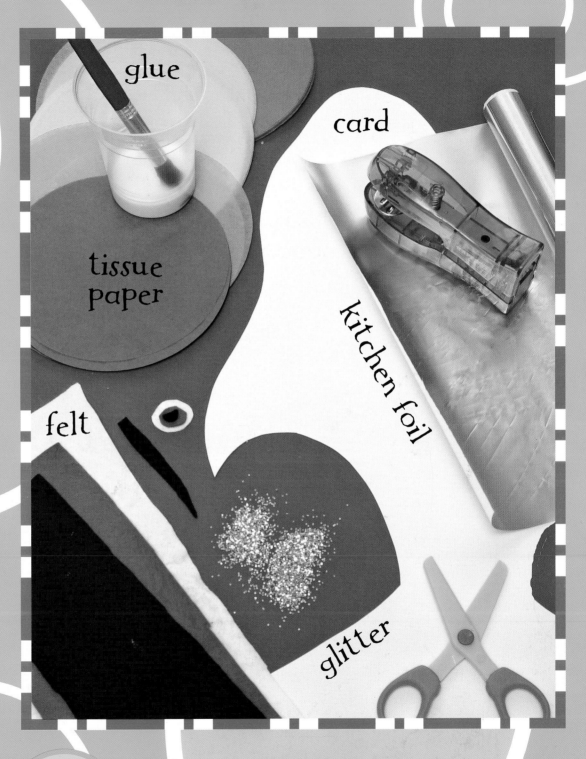

glue

card

tissue paper

kitchen foil

felt

glitter

Tot Tip!

To keep your funky hat on, staple a length of ribbon to each side and tie it in a bow under your chin.

You can do it!

draw

Draw a large fish on card – either copy ours or design your own. Cut out your fish and use it as a template to make a second fish exactly the same.

staple or tape

Staple or tape the two fish together to make a hat. Leave enough space for your head to fit in the fish's tummy.

Ooh! Very fishy!

decorate

To decorate, make tissue-paper and kitchen-foil scales and stick them in place. Sprinkle on glitter and add felt shapes for a face.

12

Kid's talk
"This is a silly fish. Fish don't have paper tails or they get wet in the water."
Alex, age 2 ¾

Sparkly Space

Make a picture of sparkly space,
Where stars shine and twinkle
And rockets love to race.

wool

fluorescent paint

Weeee!

14

You can use...

net fabric

glue

paint

wrapping paper

wool

shiny things

fabric

black paper

pipe cleaners

shiny things

Three, two, one... Blast off!
Find out how to make
this fantastic
rocket next.

Here we go!

splatter

Start your space picture by splattering watery paint onto a piece of black paper – white and fluorescent colours look great!

stick

Cut out large wrapping-paper stars and planets. Stick them on your picture with other shiny things. Add pieces of net if you like.

glue

Glue on a fabric spaceship and stick wool or pipe cleaners around its outline. Use your artistic

Did you know?
A star is a huge ball of gas that gives off masses of light and heat. The sun is our local star.

Racy Rocket

Here's a shiny little rocket.
You can make one of your own.
Then fly it high up to the stars,
And bring it safely home.

tissue paper

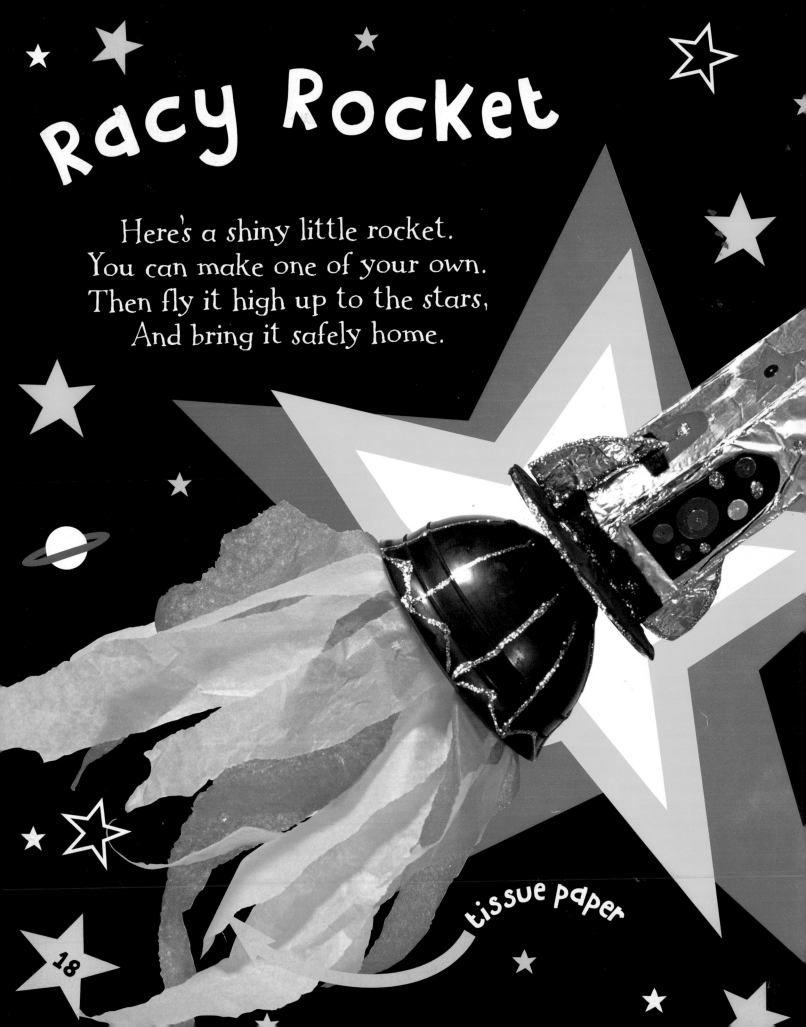

star

kitchen foil

You can use...

long box

glue

kitchen foil

glitter

coloured paper

plunger

shiny bits

scissors

stars

felt

Tot Tip!

Here's an idea to try – tape a plunger inside your rocket and then stick it on a wall tile!

You can do it!

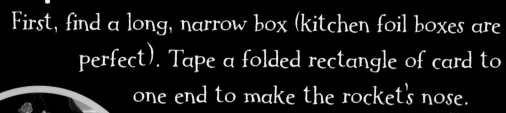

tape

First, find a long, narrow box (kitchen foil boxes are perfect). Tape a folded rectangle of card to one end to make the rocket's nose.

cover

Brush glue all over your rocket, then completely cover it with kitchen foil.

cut

Now make your rocket stand up. Cover a card semicircle with foil. Cut slits in the bottom of your rocket and slide the semicircle into them.

decorate

Decorate your rocket with cut-out coloured paper or felt shapes, sparkly stars, glitter, or other shiny bits.

rip

To make flames, rip red and yellow tissue paper into long strips. Glue the strips to the bottom of your rocket. Now take off for the stars!

Did you know?
The Apollo 11 rocket blasted Neil Armstrong into space. During this mission he became the first man ever to walk on the moon!

paint

tissue-paper lily

glitter

Monet Mastered!

Can you make a water garden
All pink and green and blue?
Monet, the great artist,
Liked to do this too!

You can use...

cardboard tube

paint

glitter

cork

sequins

tissue paper

paper

felt

Dress up your flowers with bits of fabric or shiny paper. Here's a lovely vase of flowers to make next.

Here are lovely flowers! Find out how to make them on page 26

How to make it!

paint

Paint a big sheet of paper with different shades of blue so it looks like water. Blob on paint with a cork to add texture.

staple

For the lilies, cut out circles of tissue paper. Lay about five circles on top of each other, then fold them in half and staple the middle of the fold.

scrunch

Cut zigzags on the edges of the lilies, if you like, then open them out, and scrunch each tissue circle separately. Stick the lilies on the water.

cut

Cut out a lily pad and frog shapes from paper or felt. Glue them on your picture.

finish

To finish, stick on glitter, sequins, and paper tadpoles. Print frogspawn circles with a cardboard tube and dab paint in the middle.

24

Did you know?
Monet painted many pictures of the water lilies that grew in his garden. He showed how they looked at different times of day.

Flower Power

net fabric

garden cane

plastic bottle

This lovely vase of flowers
Is colourful and bright.
Stand it on the windowsill
And it will look just right!

You can use...

glitter

tissue paper

shiny things

felt

shiny paper

garden canes

pipe cleaners

net fabric

Tot Tip! You can make the vase from a plastic bottle or plastic cup. It's waterproof and perfect for holding real flowers, too.

You can do it!

twist

First make the flower stalks. Glue green tissue paper onto garden canes. Twist it round and round, and mould it with your hands – this is messy and such fun! Tape on felt leaves.

pinch

For each flower, pile up about five circles of tissue paper (and net fabric or shiny paper). Pinch them together in the middle. Staple one end of a pipe cleaner to the pinched part of your flower. Twist the rest round one of your flower stalks.

decorate

For the vase, cut the bottom off a plastic bottle. Decorate it with pieces of tissue paper, felt shapes, glitter, and other shiny things. Then add your flowers.

28

Kid's talk
"Flowers are
like rainbows."
Heather, age 3

City Stickers

shiny
paper

If you go
To the city
For something
To buy,
You'll see that
The buildings
Go up
To the sky.
So find
Lots of boxes
And plenty
Of glue,
And make
An amazing
City view!

glitter

box

You can use...

button

paper

boxes

tubes

cotton reels

fabric

glitter

buttons

kitchen foil

paint

Tot Tip!

Good boxes to use: kitchen foil boxes, soap boxes, food packaging boxes.

I work in the city. Make me next!

Here We go!

choose

This project is such fun to do! Start by choosing a few long boxes or tubes to make into buildings.

paint

Paint the boxes in all sorts of colours. Just make them look as lovely as you can!

stick

Now stick things onto the boxes to make doors and windows. Try smaller boxes, coloured paper, foil, fabric, buttons, or cotton reels. And don't forget glitter!

stick again

Stick your buildings to a stiff piece of coloured or painted card to make a city view. We made ours into a night-time view with shiny stars in the sky.

32

You can use...

card

glue

box

coat-hanger

felt

tie

sponge

wool

paint

CD

I'm a chatty guy!

Tot Tip!

Don't want to use a CD? No problem. Instead, cut out a circle of card with a hole in the middle, and cover it with kitchen foil.

How to make it!

paint

Use a box for Mobile Man's body. Cut out his arms and legs from card or felt, and paint everything to look like a pin-striped suit.

glue

Cut out hands and shoes from more card or felt. Glue them to Mobile Man's arms and legs, then stick his arms and legs to his body.

cut

For Mobile Man's bald head, cut a slit in the top of his body and glue a CD in it. Stick on eyes, lashes, and a mouth made from card or felt. Tie on his tie.

glue again

To make the mobile phone, glue squares of felt or card onto a sponge. Add a strip of sponge to make an aerial.

thread

Thread wool through the CD and tie it to a coat-hanger. Make Mobile Man lift up his phone by tying more wool around it and the coat-hanger.

Did you know?
The first mobile phones
were about as big
as briefcases!

India the Elephant

Guess what India's made from.
Can you tell by looking?
Here's a clue – it's something
We sometimes use for cooking.

You can use...

glue

food colouring

card

glitter

uncooked rice

Saris are worn in India. Make one next!

Tot Tip! You can use any kind of rice for your picture – just make sure it's uncooked.

You can do it!

colour

First, dye your rice with food colouring – fill a few bowls with uncooked rice and stir a different food colouring into each. Keep the colours separate.

draw

Draw a picture on card. Copy our elephant, or draw a building, a flower, or anything you like. Brush glue over one area or shape in your picture.

sprinkle and shake

Sprinkle one colour of rice over the glue and shake off the excess. Glue, sprinkle, and shake again for the other areas of your picture – and if you want a sparkly picture, sprinkle on glitter, too!

Did you know? Rice grows in very wet fields called paddy fields. These fields stay wet as they are flooded by rain or river water.

Smart Sari

stencilled print

fabric

To make this lovely sari dress, here's what you have to do. Print stencils on some fabric, then wrap it right round you!

You can use...

fabric

sponge

card

paint

Tot Tip! If you don't want to make your own stencil, you don't have to. There are plenty of designs on sale in craft and home-decorating shops.

How to make it!

make a stencil

To make your stencil, draw a design on card – simple triangles and circles work well. Cut out your design.

tape

Tape about three metres of fabric to a table or the floor. Tape your stencil to the fabric, then start decorating!

dab

Use a sponge to dab a little paint over the stencil holes. Remove the stencil to see your design. Repeat as often as you like.

wrap

When your sari is dry, try it on! Wrap it around you like a skirt, then throw the end of the fabric over one shoulder.

Nellie's Knowledge

I've been teaching my art class to children for over ten years. Along the way, I've discovered a few tips that make the classes brilliant fun – and help bring out the creativity in all of us!

Organisation

It's good to have all the things you need before you start. But if you haven't got something, just improvise and use something else!

Inspiration

Look at all sorts of bits and bobs. What can you make them into? Challenge yourself and be inspired!

Colour magic

Mixing colours is magic for children! Let them discover how blue and red make purple, or blue and yellow make green.

Making mess

Art is a messy business! Just put down lots of newspaper, relax, and create. It's worth it!

Encouragement

Encouragement is great for building confidence and creativity: one hundred percent encouragement equals one hundred percent creativity!

Positive attitude

We're positive! In my art classes we never say we can't do something because we simply can!

Making choices

Children's concentration is greatest when they choose the things they want to make. They make their own decisions from the start and they see them through.

Frame it!

Show off your fabulous pictures! Make simple frames using my favourites – tissue paper and loads of glitter!

47

Now frame it! Goodbye!